SERBIAN ANIMAL COLORING BOOK

35 SWEET ANIMALS TO COLOR

WAI CHEUNG

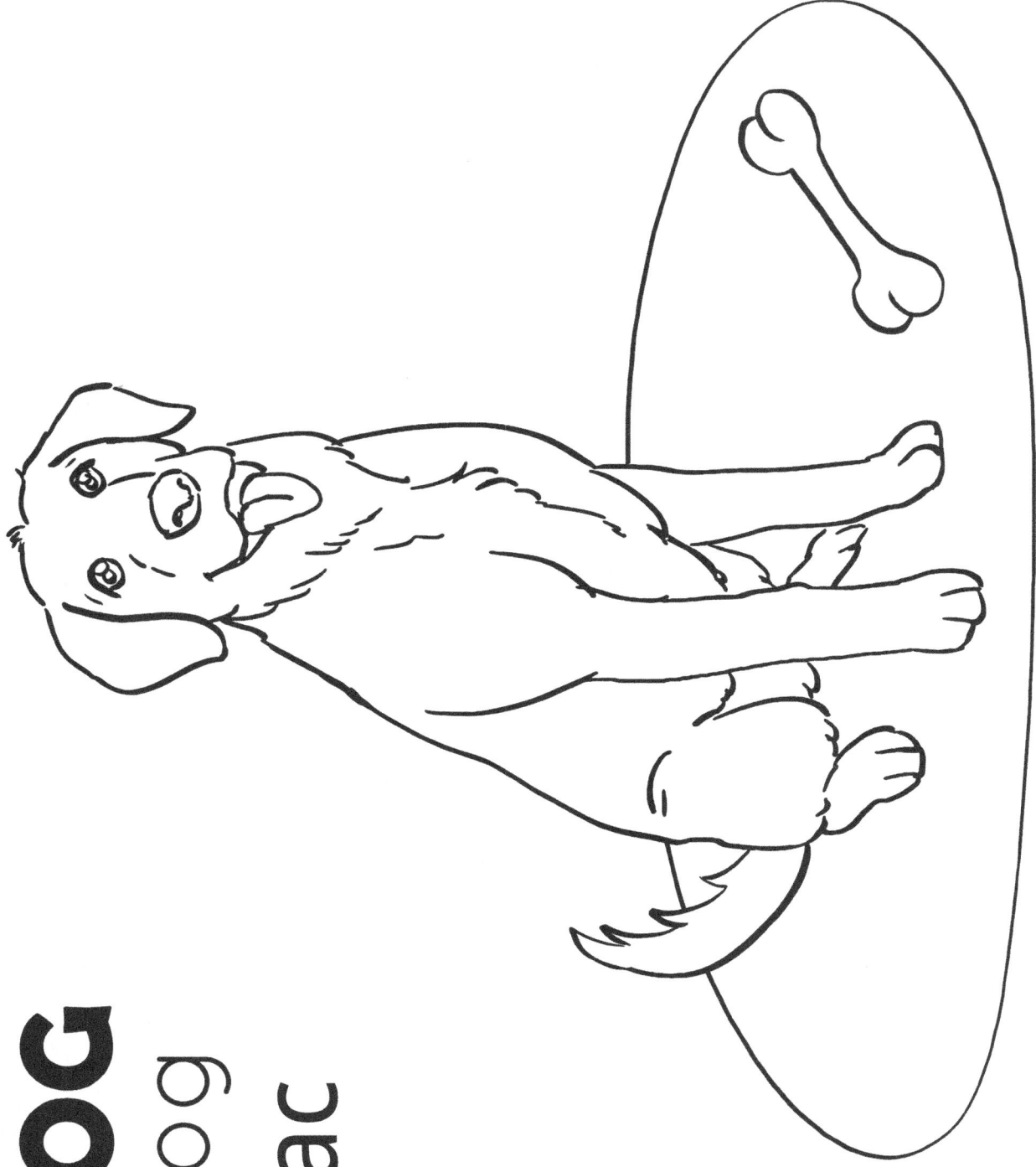

DOG
dog
пас

TIGER
tiger
тигар

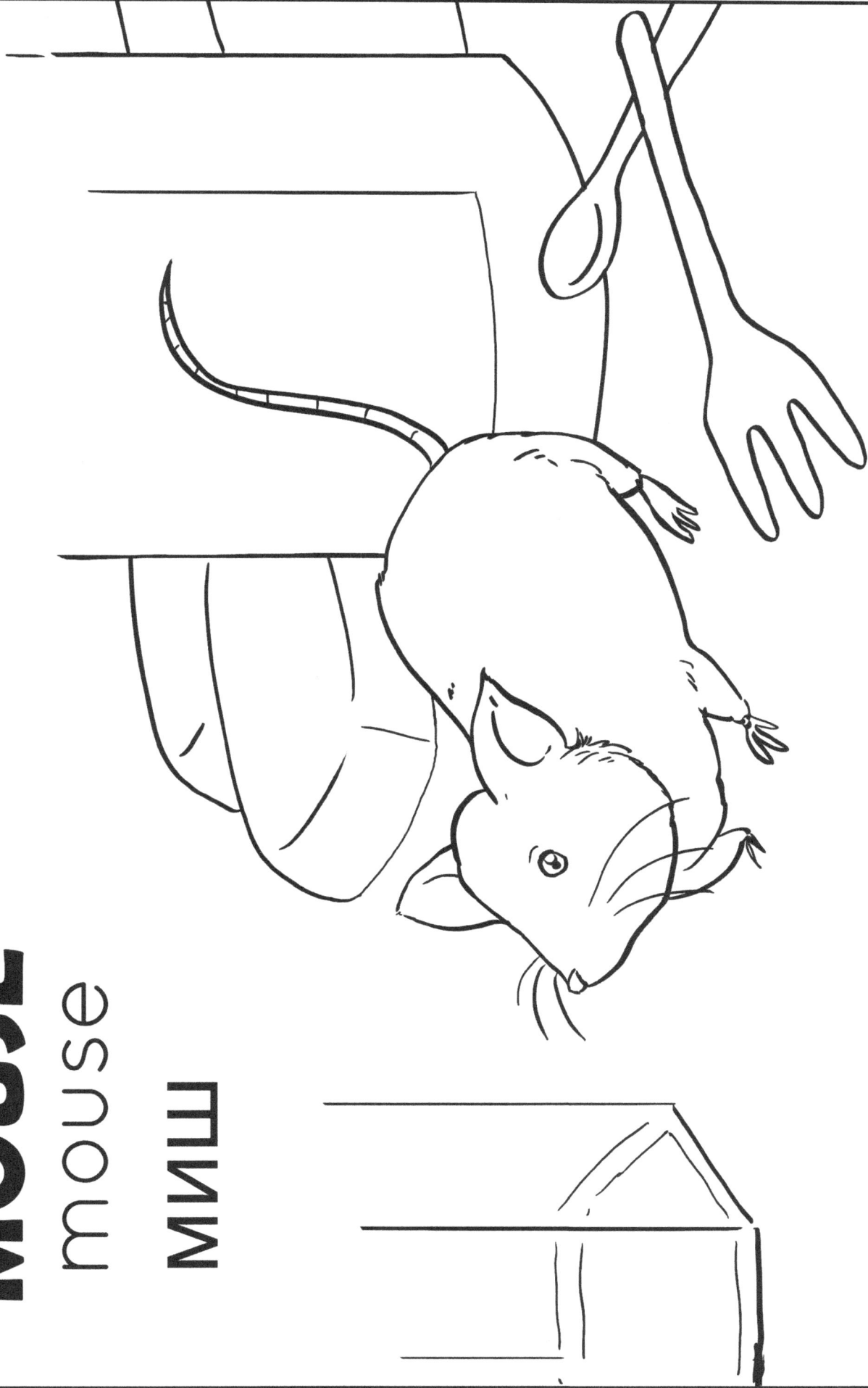

MOUSE
mouse
МИШ

DONKEY
donkey
магарац

SHEEP
sheep
овца

CHICKEN
chicken
кокошка

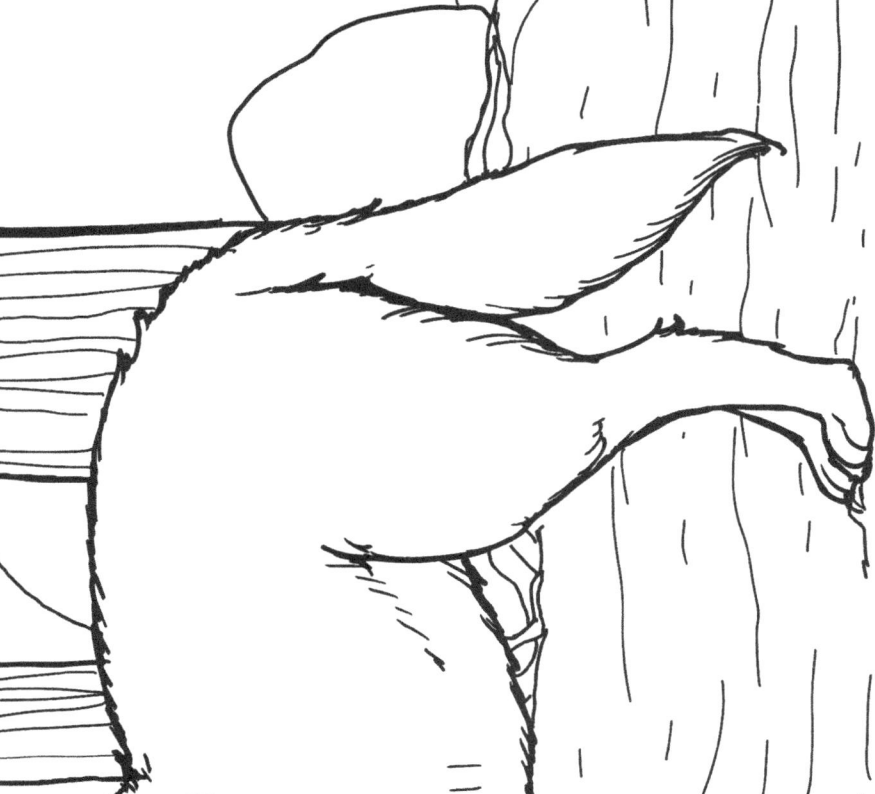

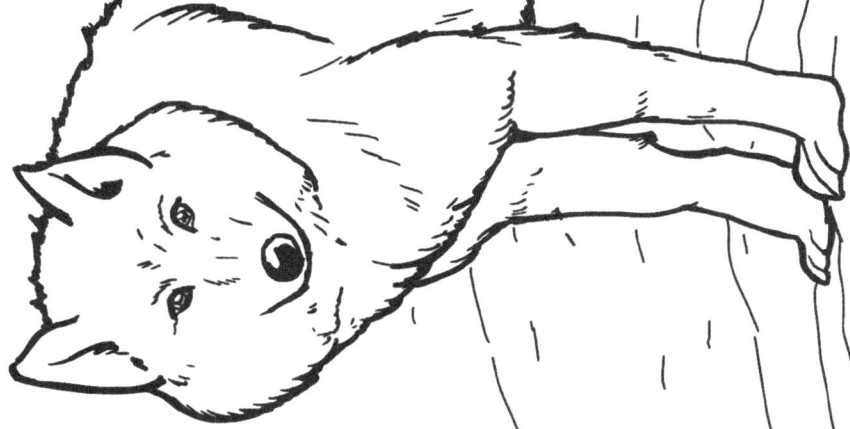

WOLF
wolf
ВУК

RACOON
racoon

ракун

ZEBRA
zebra
зебра

EAGLE
eagle
opao

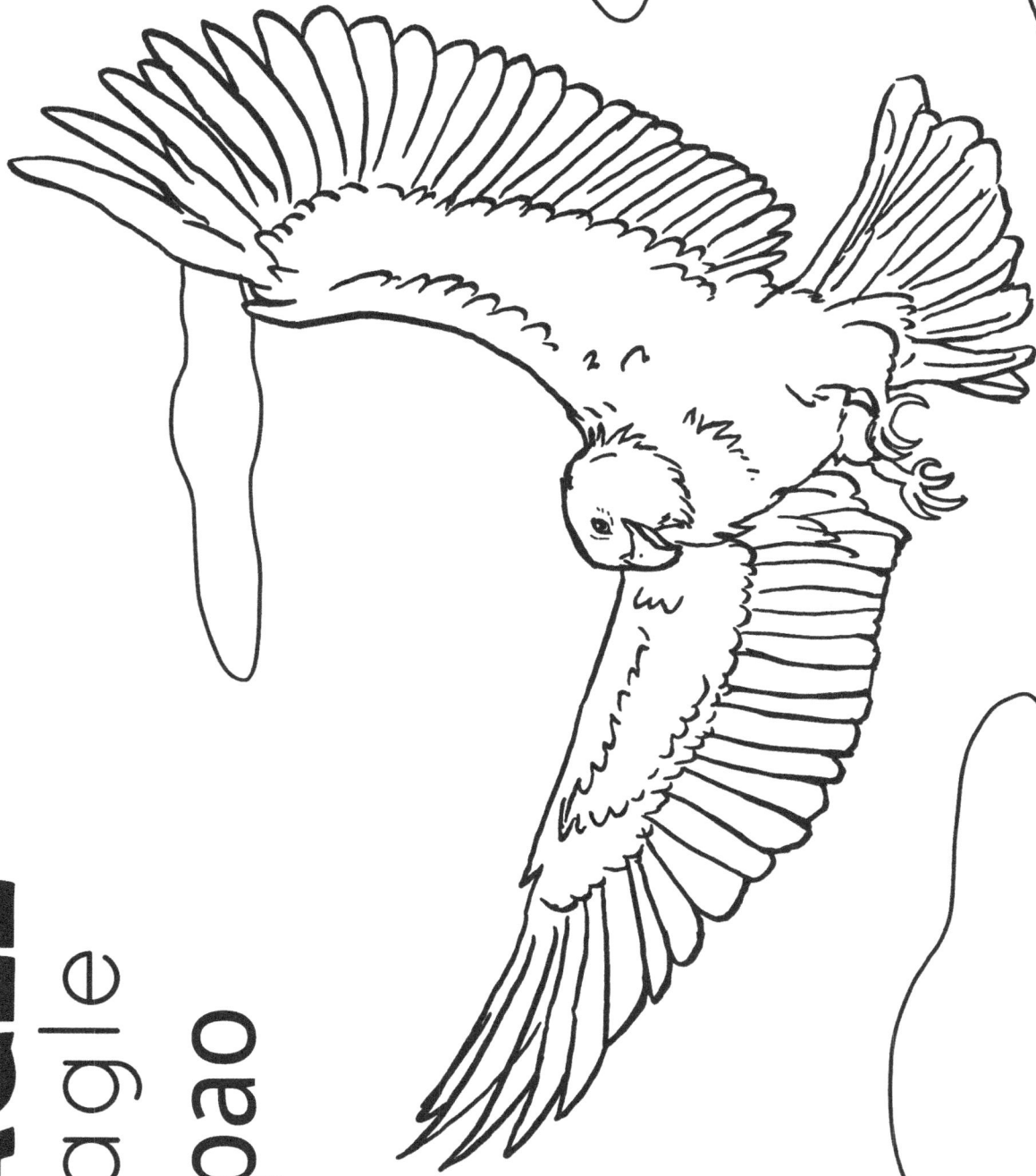

SQUIRREL
squirrel
веверица

HAMSTER
hamster
хрчак

PIG
pig
свиња

COW
COW
Крава

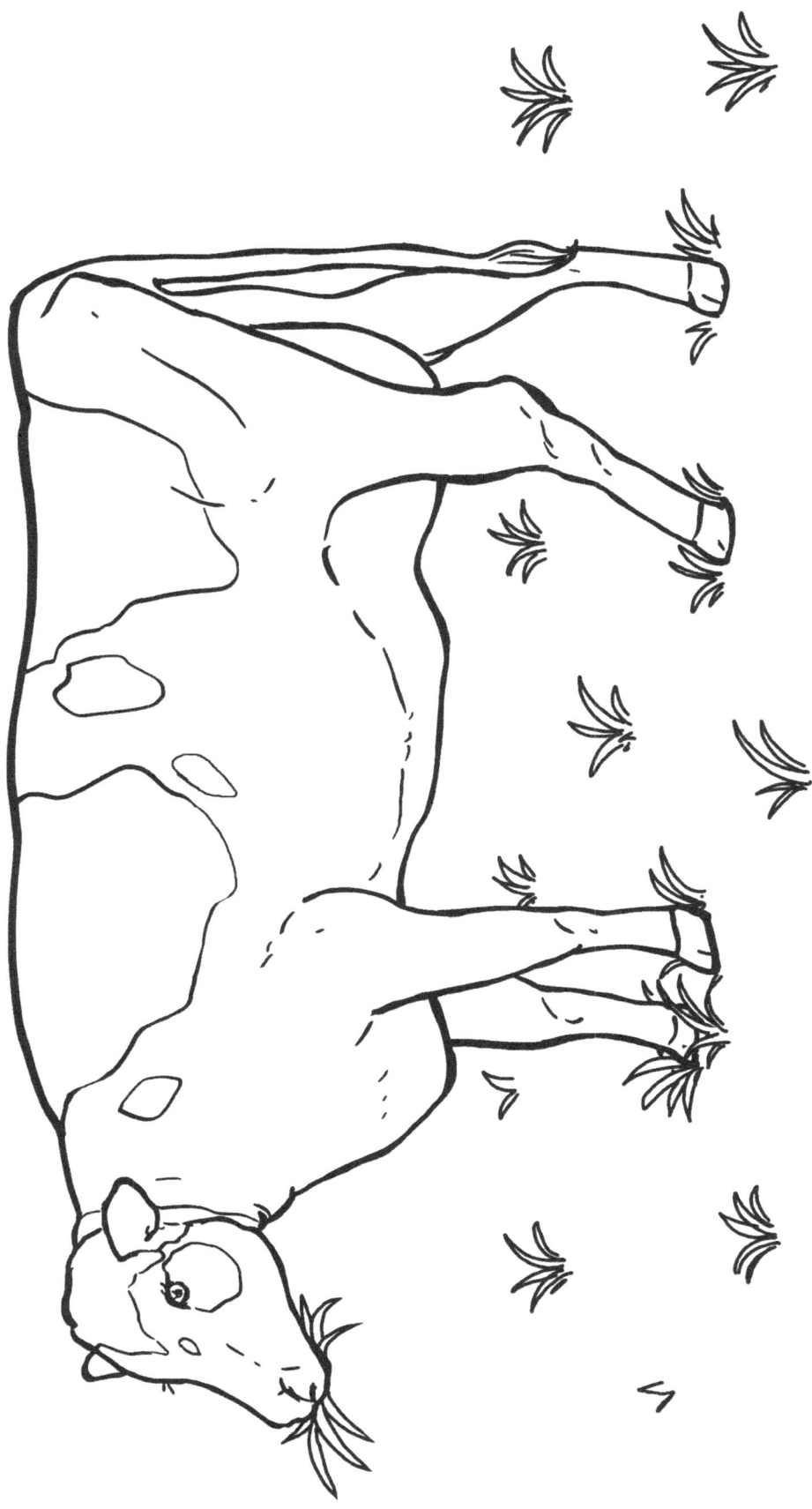

LION
lion
лав

FOX
fox

лисица

MONKEY
monkey
мајмун

ELEPHANT
elephant
слон

BEAR
bear
медвед

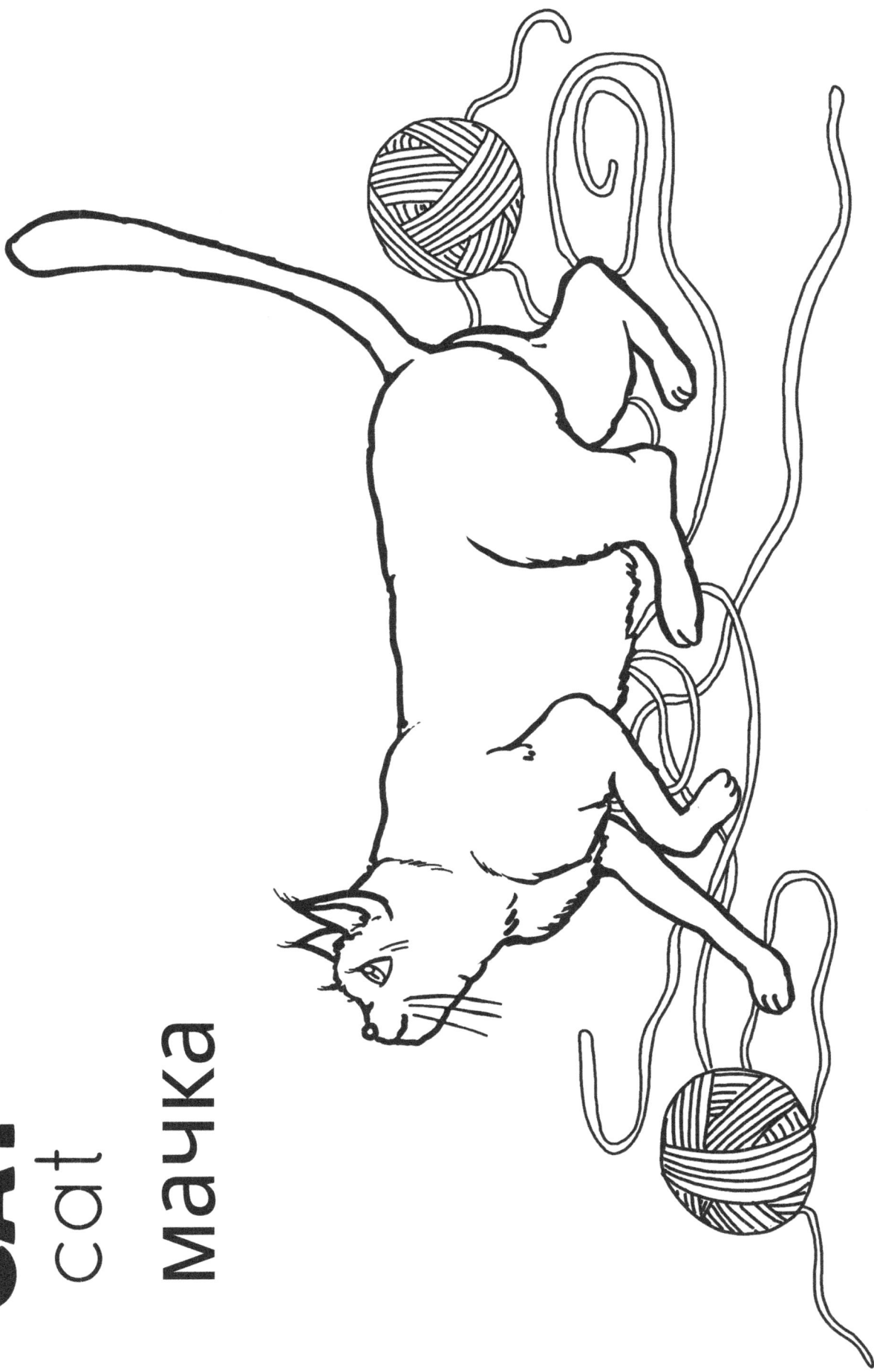

CAT
cat
мачка

PANDA
panda
панда

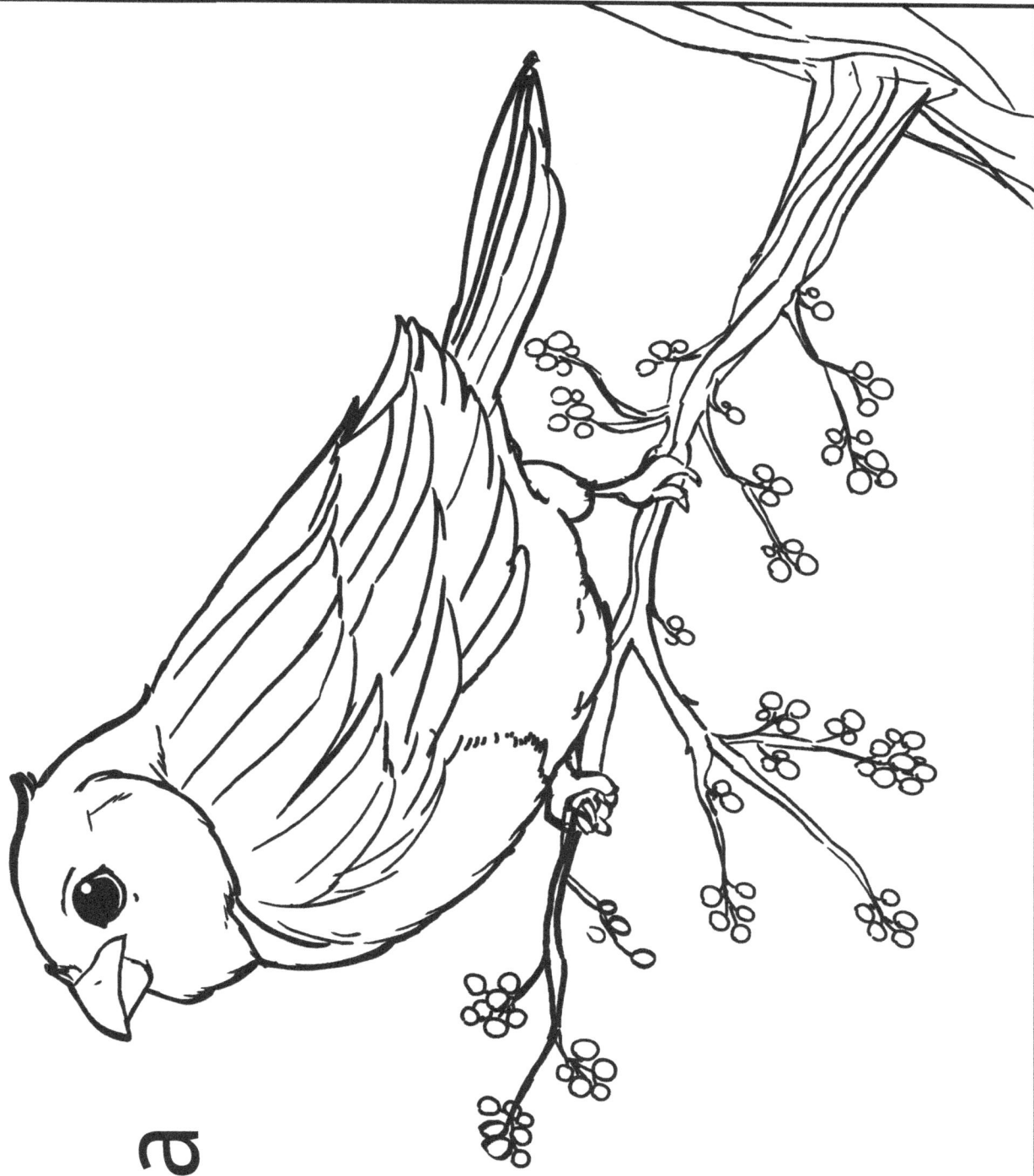

BIRD
bird
птица

FISH
fish
рыба

FROG
frog
жаба

DOLPHIN
dolphin
дельфин

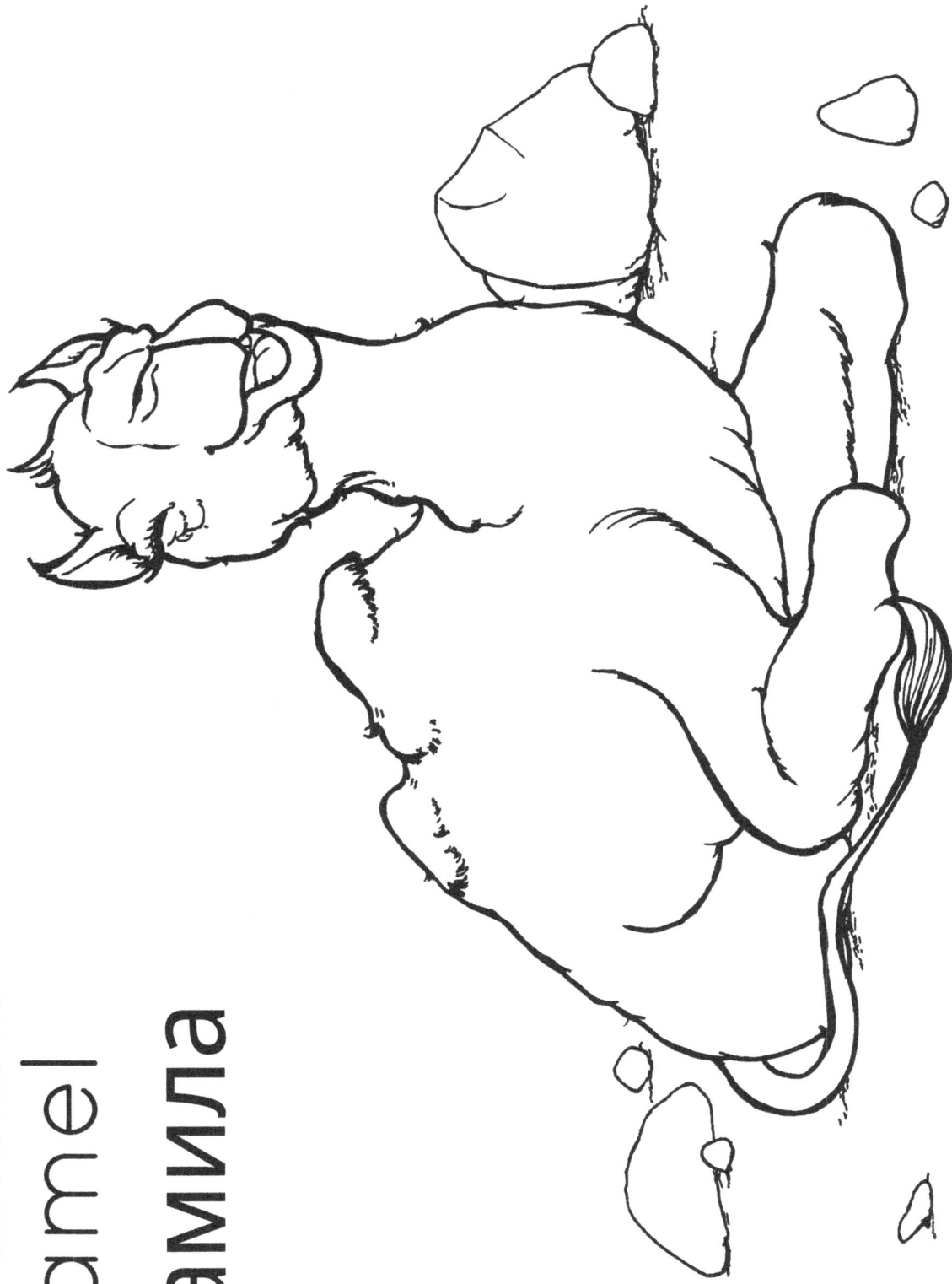

CAMEL
camel
камила

RABBIT
rabbit
зец

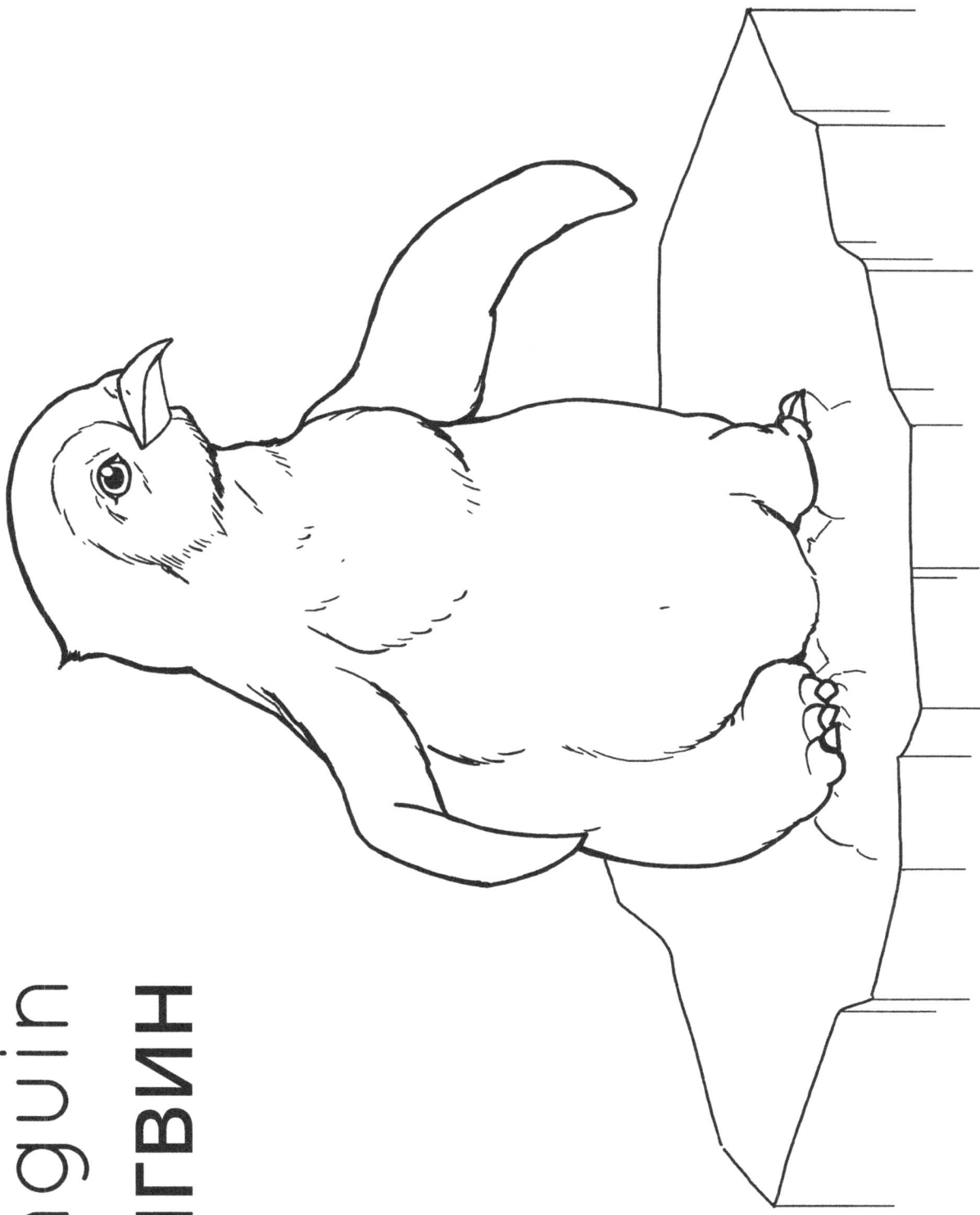

PENGUIN
penguin
ПИНГВИН

DEER
deer
јелен

OWL
owl

COBa

HORSE
horse
конь

CROCODILE
crocodile

крокодил

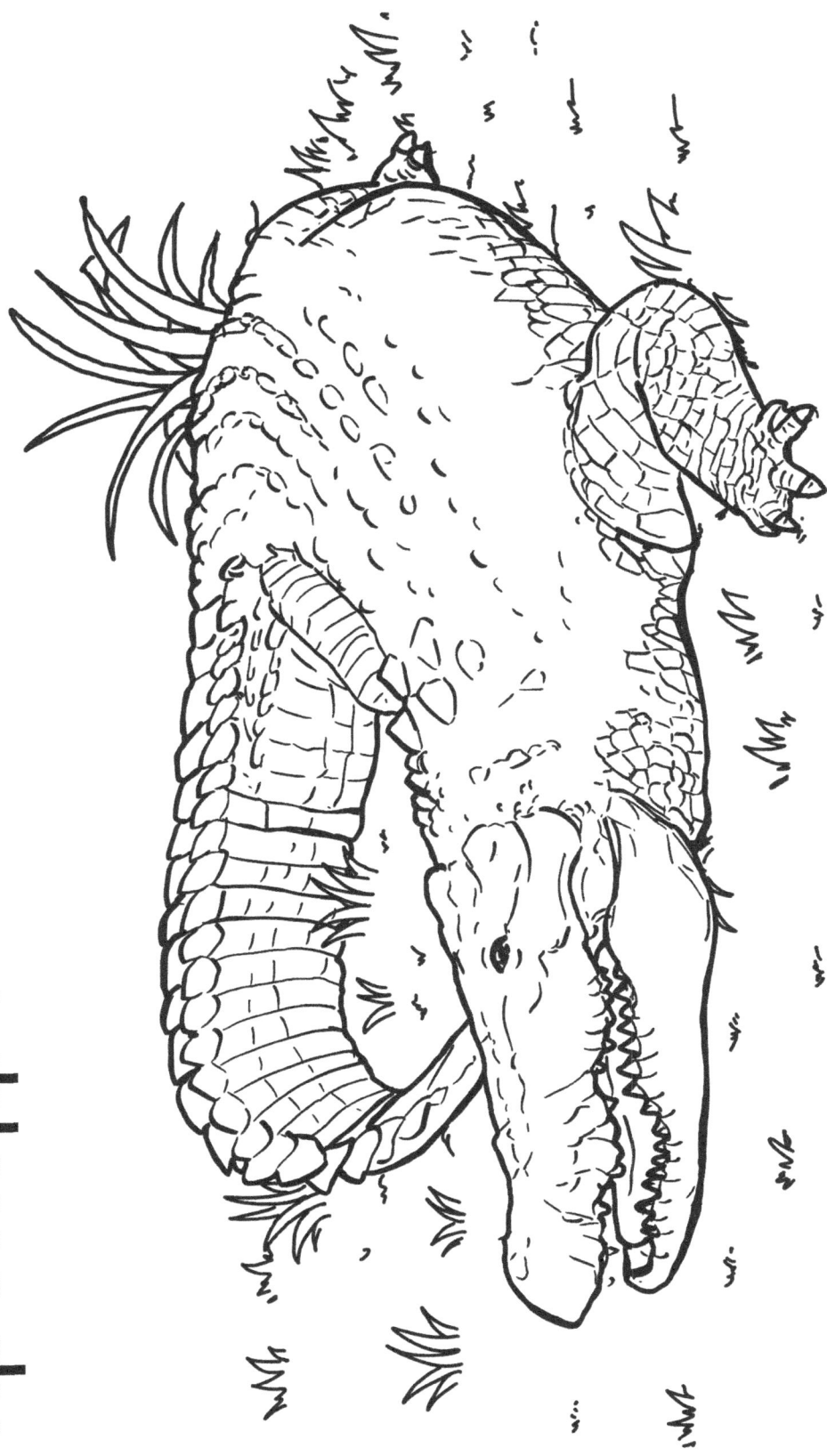

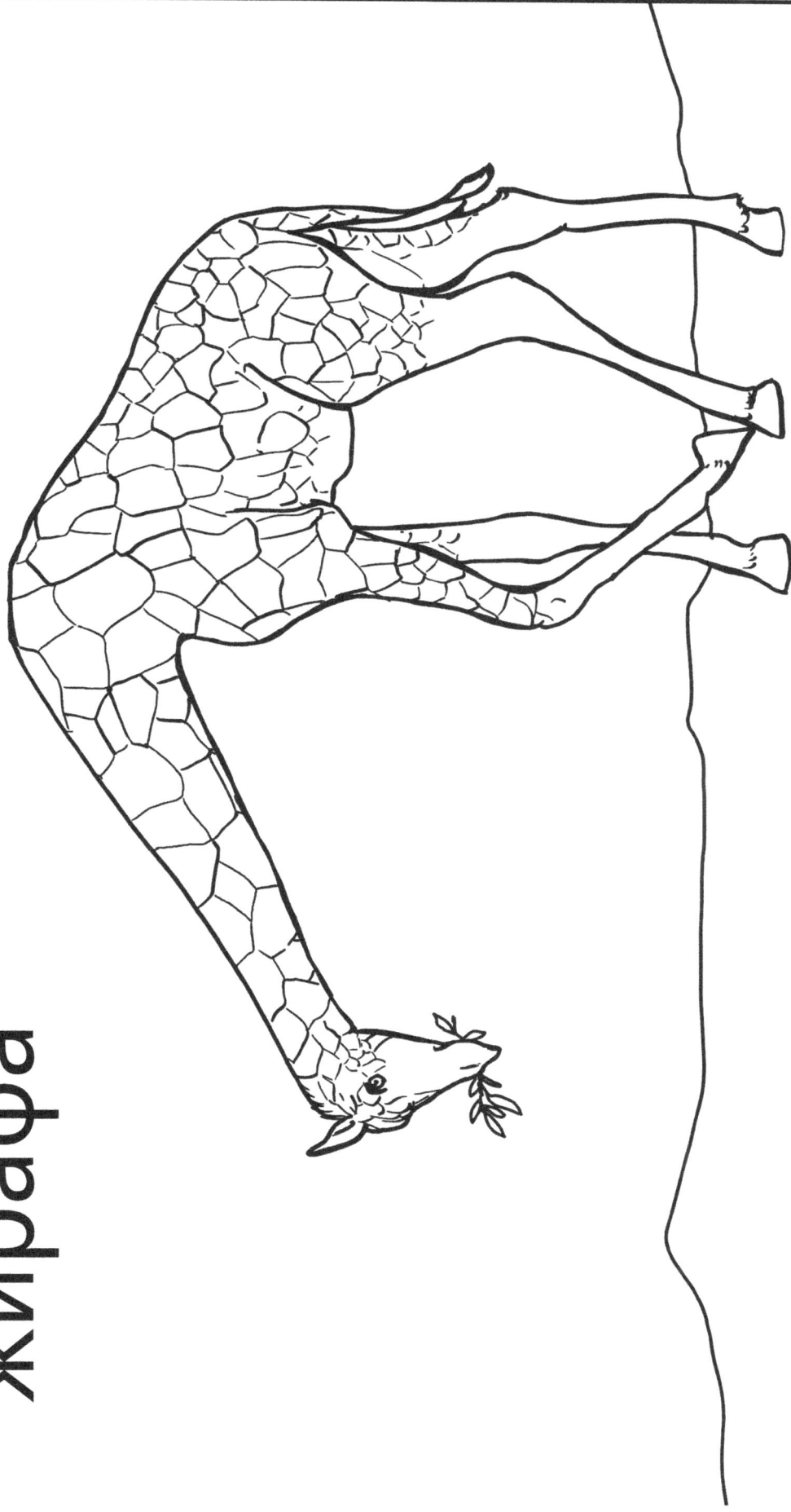

GIRAFFE
giraffe
жирафа

RHINO
rhino
Носорог

KANGAROO
kangaroo
кенгур

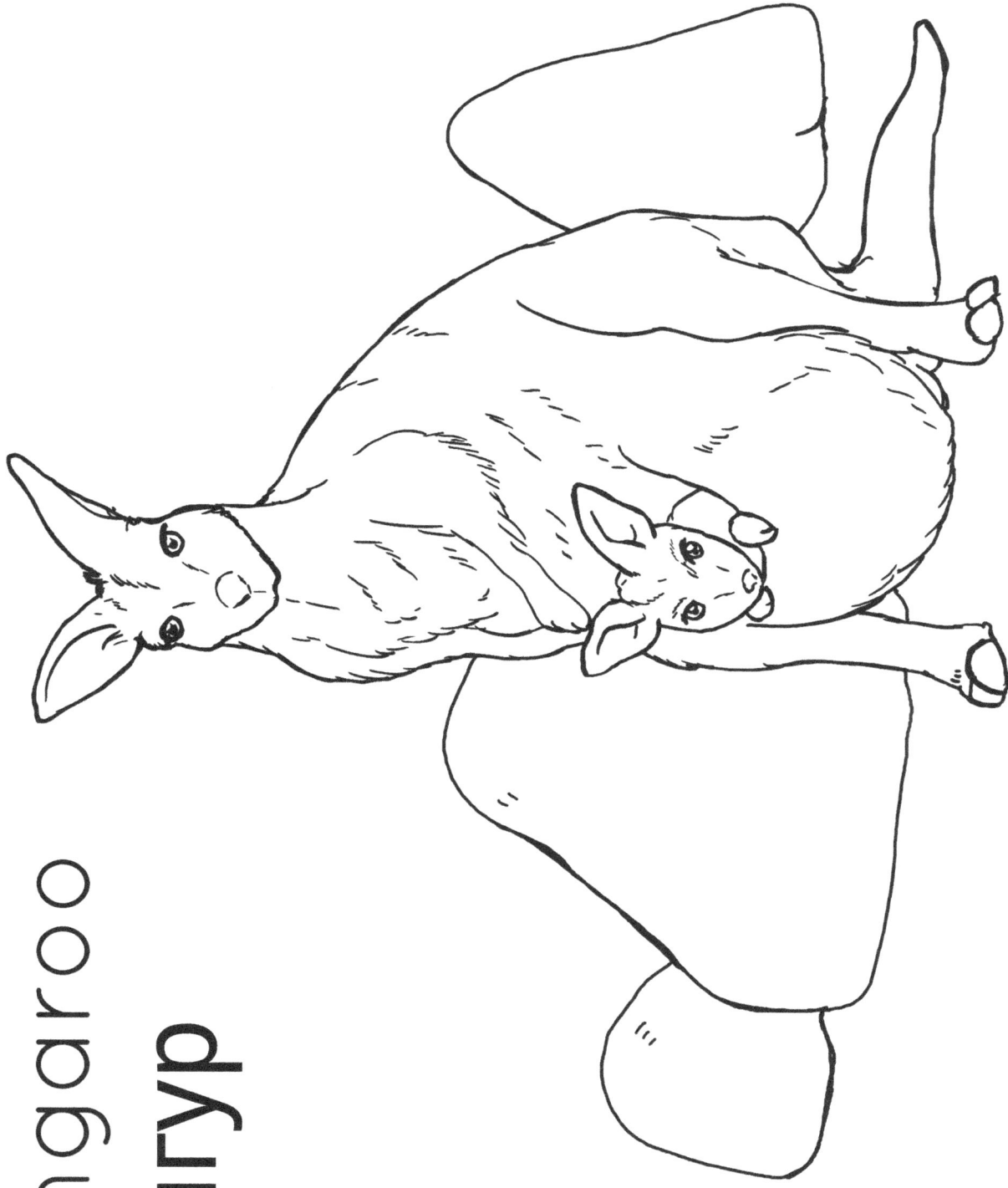

Made in the USA
Las Vegas, NV
11 January 2024